MOUNTAIN SURVIVOR'S GUIDE

MOUNTAIN SURVIVOR'S GUIDE

Rory Storm

Illustrated by Mei Lim

Scholastic Inc.

New York   Toronto   London   Auckland   Sydney
Mexico City   New Delhi   Hong Kong   Buenos Aires

ISBN 0-439-32854-3

12 11 10 9 8 7 6 5 4 3   2 3 4 5 6/0

Printed in the U.S.A.   40
First Scholastic printing, September 2001

CONTENTS

WARNING!

This guide is for learning about extreme survival situations. The techniques are not suitable for use at home and are only to be used in real emergencies.

Rory

SO YOU WANNA BE A MOUNTAIN SURVIVOR?

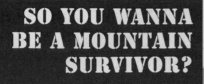

SO YOU WANNA BE A MOUNTAIN SURVIVOR?

Do you have a favorite place in all the world where you feel at your very best? Is there any particular kind of landscape that inspires and motivates you?

Well, if I had to make a choice, although it would be a close call, I'd probably say that the mountains are my spiritual home. Mountain scenery makes me feel free and alive and I find it at once awe-inspiring and humbling. Much as I revel in their beauty, I also know that mountains are dangerous and unpredictable and you must never underestimate their ability to snuff out human life in a second.

This is why all Special Forces units do part of their training and their test weeks in the hills — because it is such a difficult environment in which to survive. But survive you must and with some of the skills you'll pick up in this book, you too will have a better chance of being a mountain survivor if the situation ever arises.

BE PREPARED

Skill alone is not enough. It takes a certain type of person to be a mountain survivor. You're facing some of the harshest elements in the world, so what kind of personal attributes do you think you might need to get through a mountain ordeal? I hope you include tenacity, courage, inner strength, and resourcefulness on your list of qualities.

But there's one characteristic you probably didn't get — more so than in any other environment, planning and forethought are essential in the mountains and this quality can save lives. In the case of the two men who were polar bear hunting in Greenland, this was definitely so. They were out hunting bears on their snowmobile when the machine broke through the ice. The passenger pulled his friend, the driver, from the icy water but, after only a few paces, he died. The second man staggered the long distance back to the hut. He'd lost his gloves in the accident so his hands were badly frostbitten. Thankfully, he had left a match sticking out of the matchbox, ready to light next to a laid fire. Did you know that a simple task like getting a match from out of a closed box and striking it is almost impossible when your hands are numb with cold? He managed to light a fire and he survived his ordeal but it was probably that one simple act of planning that saved his life.

SURVIVAL MENTALITY

As in all survival situations, it is attitude that often separates those who survive from those who perish. If you are determined to come through the ordeal and you believe whole-heartedly that you will survive, then the odds change heavily in your favor.

CHAPTER ONE

A U.S. Air Force plane with eighteen men on board was flying a routine supply mission to Alert, less than 500 mi (805 km) from the North Pole when it clipped the top of a hill on its approach. Rescuers knew precisely where the plane had crashed but there were no helicopters available and it was impossible to reach them by ground.

One man had broken his back but the other crew members made a makeshift shelter and waited. A storm blew up and, with the high windchill factor, the beleaguered crew were exposed to temperatures of −94°F (−70°C). It was thirty-two hours before rescuers arrived. Remarkably, thirteen of the original eighteen were still alive. The others had died of hypothermia. Survivors from this horrendous plane crash all confirmed that it was a positive mental attitude and the will to live that got them through . . . their sense of humor and group singing helped as well.

WHAT TO EXPECT

In *Mountain Survivor's Guide*, we look at ways to provide yourself with the lifesaving essentials of shelter and warmth so you can endure the frozen conditions of a mountain survival situation. You'll also want to avoid the many dangers that are constantly lurking in the mountains, so we'll explore tactics for dealing with anything from avalanches and crevasses to ways of preventing attacks from mountain lions.

Once you've tucked these basic mountain survivor's skills under your combat belt, you'll have an opportunity to read about the brave souls who have had to employ these techniques for real. The courageous stories of real-life mountain and avalanche survivors plus the valiant tales of mountain rescuers will definitely inspire you, and who knows ... you may even pick up enough tricks along the way to help you in answering the "what if" scenarios later in the book.

And just when you thought it was all over, there's another chance to exercise your "little gray cells" once again with the Mountain Survivor's Brain Teaser, in which you're invited to come up with your very own survival plan to save you and your companions.

A HELPING HAND

In spite of the best-laid plans and stoutest heart, help sometimes comes from the most unlikely quarters. Take, for instance, the case of ten-year-old Josh Carlisle who, in March 1996, wandered away from his home in Cassville, Missouri, into the surrounding woods one cold spring morning. When temperatures fell to 2°F (−16°C) and he had still not returned, his mother, Jenny, raised the alarm. Police and local volunteers spent the next seventy-two hours searching the densely wooded hills. Hopes were fading when one of the search party heard a pair of wild dogs barking and he saw a body lying next to them. These large wild dogs had apparently adopted Josh and kept him warm during his trial. Apart from slight frostbite, he was otherwise unharmed. Nature can be cruel but, perversely, it sometimes sends us deliverance.

Luck was definitely on Josh's side and you must hope that it will bless you, too, if you ever find yourself in a mountain survival situation.

But for now, let's see what we can do to make our own luck, shall we?

ARE YOU A MOUNTAIN SURVIVOR?

ARE YOU A MOUNTAIN SURVIVOR?

So you think you could handle yourself pretty well in the mountains, huh? Well that's good to hear, but before we start this adventure together — and before you flick to the pulse-racing real-life stories — let's just establish how much you really know, shall we?

I'll let you in on a little secret . . . it doesn't really matter if you flunk this test because by the end of this book, you'll know so much great stuff about mountain survival that even I'd join you on an expedition into the hills any day.

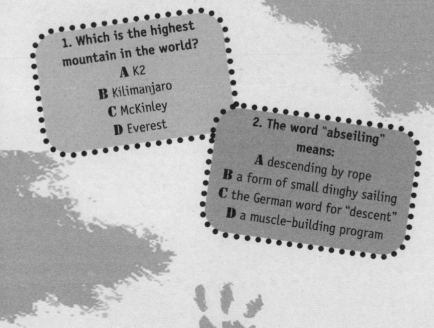

1. Which is the highest mountain in the world?
   A K2
   B Kilimanjaro
   C McKinley
   D Everest

2. The word "abseiling" means:
   A descending by rope
   B a form of small dinghy sailing
   C the German word for "descent"
   D a muscle-building program

3. A "crevasse" is:

A a small crack in a rock that can be used as a handhold

B a deep fissure that opens up in ice

C a silk scarf worn around the neck

D a hinged metal oval device for clipping you to ropes, etc.

4. In the event of an avalanche, you should:

A try to outrun it

B ski downhill and out of its path as quickly as possible, looking for something to hide behind

C try to surf on the crest of the snow-wave

D stand very still and hope it goes past you

5. If the plane you were traveling on crashed into the side of a mountain, survivors should:

A stay near the wreckage

B go out one at a time to look for help

C climb up the mountain to get away from falling debris/explosions

D stay in their seats

6. If a member of your party falls down a rock face, it takes an average of how many people to manually haul him/her back up using a rope?

A 1

B 2

C 3

D 4

7. Belaying is a method of

A crossing a river with the aid of a stick

B descending a steep rock face using ropes

C searching for avalanche victims using a sound beacon

D helping others to climb up a rock face using ropes

8. Hypothermia is
A a water spa resort in Yugoslavia
B a hypnosis treatment for a fear of cold
C a life-threatening condition where the body temperature falls well below normal
D a suggested explanation for a group of facts or phenomena

9. The best treatment for frostbite is to:
A rub the affected area with snow
B thaw the injured area gradually with warm water
C expose the affected area to an open fire
D thaw the injured area as quickly as possible in hot water

10. Polar bears are powerful swimmers. They can stay submerged in polar waters for up to:
A 30 seconds
B 2 minutes
C 5 minutes
D 10 minutes

11. The first person to reach the South Pole was:
A Sir Robert Scott
B Sir Ranulph Fiennes
C Ernest Shackleton
D Roald Amundsen

12. The slopes of a mountain most in danger of avalanching are:
A snow-covered convex, lee slopes
B snow-covered concave, lee slopes
C ice-covered, convex slopes
D ice-covered, concave slopes

ANSWERS

So how did you do? Were the questions tougher or easier than you expected? Let's see, shall we? Give yourself one point for every correct answer (and no cheating):

1d Everest in Nepal is the highest mountain in the world at 29,028 ft (8,848 m) closely followed by K2 in Kashmir-Sinkiang at 28,250 ft (8,611 m). Mount McKinley (20,320 ft/6,194 m) is the highest mountain in the U.S. and Kilimanjaro in Tanzania at 19,340 ft (5,895 m) is the highest mountain in Africa.

2a Abseiling is a very quick way to descend a rock face using a rope, but it's not as easy as it is made to look in movies. It should only be attempted under the supervision of experienced professionals who will act as anchormen — and then it can be great fun!

3b Crevasses are a mountaineer's biggest nightmare, as they can open up unexpectedly in the ice causing disasters. If you chose a) you were probably thinking of a crevice, which is indeed useful as a handhold when climbing. A cravat, which is a silk scarf, is probably not going to do you much good in freezing conditions, although you'd look very good, I'm sure. The metal device you're thinking of is a carabiner.

4b Skiing down and traversing out of the avalanche's path is the best bet. If you can't get out of its way, try to find something solid to shelter behind. You have to be very lucky to outrun an avalanche, which can travel at speeds of up to 200 mph (322 kph). Surfing may sound outlandish, but if caught in an avalanche, using a backstroke action with your arms has been known to keep victims on top or near the surface of the snow. Never stand still in the face of an avalanche — you'll be doomed.

5a It's much easier for rescuers to spot wreckage than to find individuals, although you should keep a healthy distance in case the plane bursts into flames (so it's definitely not recommended to stay in your seat). If you are going to move away, go down the mountain toward warmth and shelter, never up. And if you do send out reconnaissance parties, the golden rule is never to go alone.

6c On average, it takes three strong men to manhandle a body up a rock face. So you'd better get in shape.

7d Belaying is a safe way to rock climb using ropes. The other answers sounded quite convincing, though, didn't they?

8c Yep, hypothermia — the cold is a killer on the mountains. If you chose d) you're probably thinking of hypothesis and if you chose either a) or b), you're probably nuts!

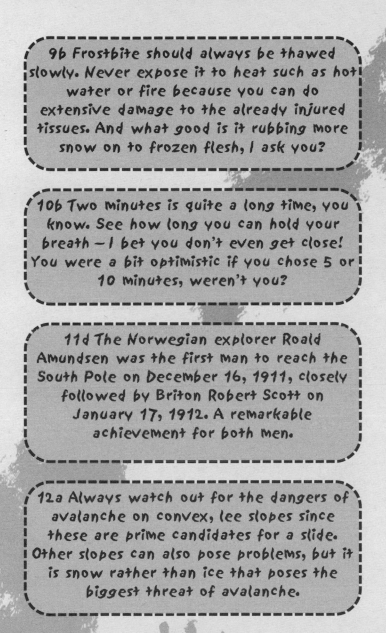

9b Frostbite should always be thawed slowly. Never expose it to heat such as hot water or fire because you can do extensive damage to the already injured tissues. And what good is it rubbing more snow on to frozen flesh, I ask you?

10b Two minutes is quite a long time, you know. See how long you can hold your breath — I bet you don't even get close! You were a bit optimistic if you chose 5 or 10 minutes, weren't you?

11d The Norwegian explorer Roald Amundsen was the first man to reach the South Pole on December 16, 1911, closely followed by Briton Robert Scott on January 17, 1912. A remarkable achievement for both men.

12a Always watch out for the dangers of avalanche on convex, lee slopes since these are prime candidates for a slide. Other slopes can also pose problems, but it is snow rather than ice that poses the biggest threat of avalanche.

SCORING

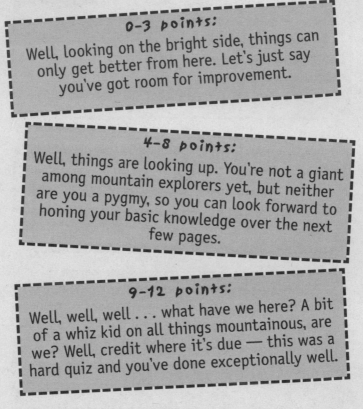

0-3 points:

Well, looking on the bright side, things can only get better from here. Let's just say you've got room for improvement.

4-8 points:

Well, things are looking up. You're not a giant among mountain explorers yet, but neither are you a pygmy, so you can look forward to honing your basic knowledge over the next few pages.

9-12 points:

Well, well, well . . . what have we here? A bit of a whiz kid on all things mountainous, are we? Well, credit where it's due — this was a hard quiz and you've done exceptionally well.

So, did you leap to the dizzy heights of success like a mountain goat or are you scurrying like a gopher in the foothills of despair? Whatever your results, don't be downhearted, because there's always more you can learn as you work your way through the book.

But now I think it's time we got down to some real work, don't you?

BASIC MOUNTAIN SURVIVAL SKILLS

BASIC MOUNTAIN SURVIVAL SKILLS

It's hard to think of any good reason why you might find yourself alone on a mountain. Even experienced walkers, climbers, and mountaineers only venture out in a party of at least two. Having said that, even the best of us can get into trouble on occasion and you may find yourself in a desperate situation high in the mountains through no fault of your own or of anyone else. Typically, you might become separated from your group or, worst-case scenario, your plane could crash into the mountainside.

In these desperately dangerous situations, you must rely on your survival knowledge, your strength of character and determination, initiative, teamwork (where applicable), and, dare I say it, luck.

Nonetheless, you can increase your chances of survival in the inhospitable and fickle mountain environment by making sure you are always well prepared before you set off into the hills. As I've said before, mountains deserve respect and if you don't heed this warning, you may one day be forced to regret your cavalier attitude. Unless you find yourself unlucky enough to be unexpectedly dumped in the mountains by a plane crash or something of that nature, you'd be well advised to always travel with a mountain survival kit — and, like me, it will soon become second nature and you'll feel bare without a backpack.

BE PREPARED

In a survival situation, you can seldom replace or change your clothes, so it's important to choose well before you set off.

FORGET BEING A FASHION VICTIM

The major cause of death when lost in the mountains is not all the terrifying dangers that you may face from avalanche or ferocious animals, but simple hypothermia (see page 85). Humans are basically tropical animals whose bodies work best between 96°F and 102°F (35.5°C and 39°C), so you must dress properly before venturing into the hills.

If you layer your clothing you get the best mix of insulation and ventilation and these layers can then be added or removed depending upon how warm you feel. This, of course, is governed by what you're doing, i.e., activity = higher body temperature, so if you're feeling cold — run around or, better still, do some useful work.

Inner layer: The layer next to the skin should be made of a thin cotton or polypropylene material that is loose-fitting and able to draw perspiration away from the skin.

Second layer: A woolen layer with a zipper or elasticized neck and wrists should come next.

Third layer: A fleece-lined shirt or parka jacket with a hood is an ideal middle layer as it traps and creates warm "dead air" space. This layer should be easily removable.

Outer layer: This must be waterproof and windproof with a large hood. Gore-Tex or another brand of breathable material is ideal since it allows moisture out but not in.

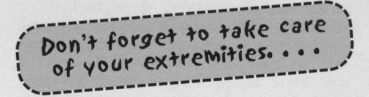

Don't forget to take care of your extremities. . . .

Did you know that you lose 47 percent of your body heat from your head? So make sure you have a good hat with pull-down earflaps to wear under your waterproof hood. In the military, we use a long woolen tube called a "headover" that can be pulled down around the neck like a scarf or up over the head and ears. I wouldn't leave home without one! Remember the old saying: If you want to get ahead, get a hat!

If your hands are too cold you can't build a shelter or fire, so never forget your gloves. Most outdoor specialists recommend a pair of fine woolen gloves with a pair of waterproof mittens over the top for extreme conditions.

It's hard to walk on numb feet so make sure you have good waterproof boots that are large enough to comfortably accommodate two pairs of socks — one thin pair under thick, knee-length ski socks.

Mountain Survivor's Tip

If you're skiing and you need to take a break, instead of getting a cold, wet backside from sitting in the snow, make yourself a comfortable seat:

Plant your skis in deep snow or a bank of snow, about 2 ft (.6 m) apart.

Place one ski pole across the bindings and put the second pole, hand-grip facing the other way, on top of it.

Presto! A seat fit for a king — well, you're off the snow anyway!

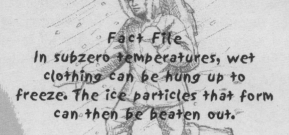

Fact File
In subzero temperatures, wet clothing can be hung up to freeze. The ice particles that form can then be beaten out.

SURVIVAL KIT

Remember to always pack the following items in your backpack when you go out into the hills and make sure you know how to use them — it's much harder if you're reading the instructions for the first time in the dark and cold. These recommendations are for low-level walking in the winter — for high-level walking — more than 1,640 ft (500 m) — extra clothing and equipment should be packed:

❄ **An extra layer of clothing**
❄ **A breathable, hooded coat**
❄ **Hat, spare socks, gloves, and mittens**
❄ **A flashlight**
❄ **Emergency rations: e.g. carbohydrates such as chocolate bars, candy, bagels, peanuts, cereal bars, trail mix, etc.**
❄ **A large, filled water bottle**

❄ A signaling device such as a small mirror or whistle (you can also use your flashlight at night)

❄ A small space blanket that has a foil-like coating, or a survival bag — in case you need to camp for the night

❄ Someone responsible in the group should bring a small first-aid kit and a heat source such as a trioxane pack — a light chemical heat source used by the army — plus some boxes of waterproof matches and a lighter

❄ Map and compass

Mountain Survivor's Tip

When packing your backpack, make sure you know where things are so you can find them easily when you need them. Food and water need to be near the top. Try to put softer items such as clothing next to your back. Put things in different-colored bags to help you find them more easily (and to keep them dry).

Mountain Survivor's Tip

If you've survived an aircraft crash in the mountains, the upturned life rafts make an excellent emergency shelter — but don't forget to secure them, because winds gust at higher altitudes.

WHEN THINGS GO WRONG

Mountains are hostile and inaccessible places, so when things go wrong, it's hard for rescuers to get to you, and salvation can take some time. This is why it's so important for you to have some idea of how you can help yourself in an emergency.

The following tips may sound obvious, but they can mean the difference between life and death when you're on an exposed mountain. Would you be able to think clearly and follow these few simple rules in an emergency?

❊ Always keep the group together. People walk at different paces so make sure the leaders don't leave the rest behind — keep one fast walker at the back so s/he can tell when the group is going too fast.

❊ Rest when the slowest member needs to, but don't get chilled.

❊ Never try to move someone who is injured. Make sure they are as comfortable as possible, warm, and have food and water. Get help as soon as possible.

❊ If an individual gets separated from the group, keep the main group together at a central rendezvous point. Always keep two or three people here. Send others off in pairs to look for the missing person — reporting back every forty-five minutes or so to see if the search has been successful. Meanwhile, one pair should have gone off to find help from the mountain rescue or other walkers.

❄ The main group should reach safety before it gets dark. You should NEVER try to get down in the dark — this is how people die on mountains. If you can get down before nightfall, alert the mountain rescue that you're down safely. If not, it's time to use the equipment that you packed that allows you to stay on the mountain in safety until there is enough light to go down safely.

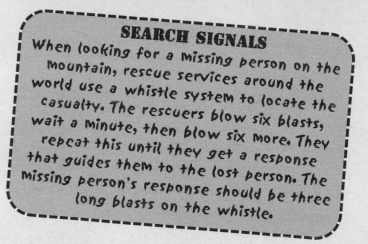

SEARCH SIGNALS

When looking for a missing person on the mountain, rescue services around the world use a whistle system to locate the casualty. The rescuers blow six blasts, wait a minute, then blow six more. They repeat this until they get a response that guides them to the lost person. The missing person's response should be three long blasts on the whistle.

MAKING A SHELTER

If it looks like you're going to have to spend at least one night on the mountain, then you are going to need some form of shelter to survive. If you don't have a tent or survival blanket, don't panic. For the resourceful, there is always something you can do to improve the situation.

NATURAL SHELTER

If you find yourself below the tree line, look for a large fir tree. Dig the snow out from around the base of the tree and pile it up around the edges to form a wall. On the side of the tree sheltered from the wind (the leeward side), make a bed from branches cut from the other side of the tree, to insulate you against the cold ground. Make sure you build your fire so that it doesn't melt the snow from overhanging branches on top of you.

SNOW SHELTER

In the event that you find yourself marooned above the tree line and with no caves to provide natural protection (assuming they don't already have occupants), you'll have to improvise and make your own shelter.

• Make a mound roughly bigger than you from your backpack or foliage or wreckage (you'll have to use your imagination here) and, if possible, cover it with a sheet of some kind (a survival blanket perhaps?).

• Now heap snow on top of the sheet and compress it firmly. Make sure the layer of snow is about 12 in (30.5 cm) thick at least (use sticks stuck in from the outside to measure thickness).

• As the compressed snow freezes, forming a hard outer layer, you can cut a hole on the leeward side (away from the wind) large enough to get out your backpack or the other contents of your mound. (If you're forced to use piled snow as the basis of your mound, just scoop this out.)

• Don't worry too much if bits of your shelter cave in—these can be easily repaired once inside.

• Leave a small hole in the roof for ventilation.

• When you enter your shelter for the night, block up the entrance with your backpack or a very large snowball! And don't forget to take your digging implements inside with you in case you have to dig yourself out in the morning.

Mountain Survivor's Tip

Building a shelter of any kind is quite hard work, believe me, and you will perspire even in freezing conditions. So take off an inner garment before you start work and replace it the moment you are tucked inside your shelter or when you stop work.

Fact File
Snow conducts heat away from the body twenty times more than leaves or branches, so always make sure you're insulated from the snow when you lie down in your shelter to sleep. Use a backpack, branches, or anything you can lay your hands on.

MAKING A FIRE

It's almost impossible to make a fire if you find yourself above the tree line and without matches or a stove pack. In this case, it's better to just try and stay warm in your shelter and think about your escape plan.

If you're among trees, even though it's snowy, you should be able to light a fire if you can find dry tinder (dried moss is excellent), kindling, and wood. Here's the basic method:

A WIGWAM FIRE

• Clear an area of snow until you have a bare earth surface, or place a platform of damp logs on the snow on which to build your fire.

- Make a small pile of kindling (twigs, small sticks, and small, dry leaves).

- Around this, build a wigwam shape with thin but longer sticks.

- Put a ball of tinder (dry grass, dead leaves, dry moss, bark which you keep dry inside your clothing — a top British Special Air Service (SAS) trick) inside the kindling. Light the tinder with a match. The kindling will soon catch.

- Once your fire is lit, it will burn fiercely. The wigwam will collapse into a pile of hot, burning embers. Now, very carefully, add more sticks.

CHAPTER THREE

Mountain Survivor's Tip

In arctic conditions, the SAS dry wet boots
by placing warm stones from around the fire
inside (carefully lifting them with a couple
of sticks). You have to check that what
emanates from your boots is steam and not
smoke or instead of nice dry boots you could
find yourself with a hole in your shoe!

GETTING DRINKING WATER

Once your supply of drinking water from your
container has run out, you'll need to find another
supply. Even though your need for water is
reduced in cold conditions, you must still drink or
you will become progressively dehydrated. When
you have access to fire and pots, your task is easy,
but if you're on your own, avoid the temptation
to simply pop snow or ice into your mouth — this
can damage the delicate membranes of the mouth
and cause dehydration. Rather, you should crush
snow into a snowball with your hands. Keep
crushing it and slowly it will start to melt — let
the melting water drip into your mouth. If you
can break some off, ice is much easier to melt
than snow — and, of course, the smaller the
piece, the faster it melts.

Mountain Survivor's Tip

Melt snow a little at a time in a pot over the fire and gradually add more. If you put a lot in at once, a hollow will form at the bottom as it melts and you'll burn your pot.

GETTING TO SAFETY

In the majority of cases, an excellent international network of mountain rescue teams means that, wherever they may be in the "developed" world, unfortunate souls lost in the mountains are often found and rescued without any long-term ill effects. However, there are occasions when the rescue services, for whatever reason, can't get to you and then it may well be that you and your fellow survivors have to walk to safety yourselves.

GOING DOWN

The sooner you get down to less exposed and warmer conditions the better. However, there are a few rules to bear in mind:

❊ **Look for worn paths or other signs of a route that may have been used by others to make your descent easier.**

❊ **When scrambling down, make sure you are facing in toward the rock.**

❊ **Avoid gullies where the risk of stone falls is greater.**

❄ If in a group, be careful to ensure that rocks loosened by those above do not knock off those below.

❄ Beware of slopes covered in scree (small, loose stones) as these can lead to a cliff that cannot be seen from the top.

❄ If climbing alone, make sure you have three points in contact with the rock at all times. (Don't put your knees on the rock, as this will unbalance you.)

❄ Finally, in poor visibility, be extra vigilant — even experienced climbers can get lost in a whiteout.

CROSSING DEEP SNOW

It is incredibly exhausting to walk in deep snow when you sink up to your knees or higher with every step. If this is the sort of terrain you'll have to cross, you'd be wise to invest a short amount of time in making some snowshoes for yourself before you set off. These spread your body weight over a larger area of snow and help you to move more quickly without sinking with every step.

• Cut a length of green sapling and keep bending it around your knee to make it pliable.

• Bend it into an arch and carefully scrape away the bark on the inside of the curve to make it more flexible.

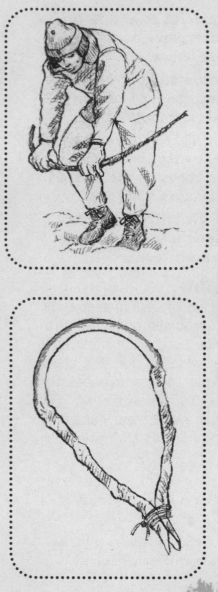

• Cut one side of both ends of the branch so that when held together, they rest flush against each other.

• Hold these ends together and bind with string to form a hoop.

- Find six short sticks and bind them in pairs at their center.
- Lash the three pairs of sticks across the hoop to support the foot.

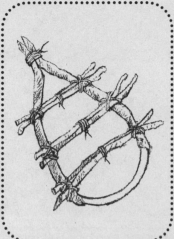

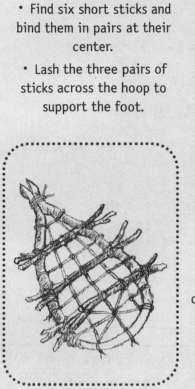

- Weave string in and around the frame and the cross-sticks to form the base of the snowshoe.

- Tie the finished snowshoe to your walking boots with string or cord.
- Repeat for the other foot.

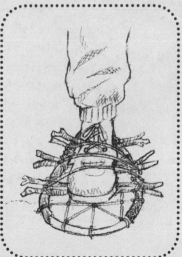

Mountain Survivor's Tip

When crossing icy slopes, you must take the utmost care. If you're in a group, you should rope yourselves together and probe ahead looking with an ice ax or long stick for crevasses (see true-life stories on page 52 for a drama involving crevasses!). This will also lend you support if you slip. If you do fall on an icy slope and you're gaining momentum, try to stick the pointed end of your ice ax or your stick into the ground and lean all your weight on it to try to break your speed and to stop you.

Survivor's Tale

In polar regions, sleds are pulled by dogs, and usually by huskies, which are perfectly suited to the polar conditions because of their thick, coarse coats and heavily furred feet.

One of the most outstanding feats of animal endurance came from two dogs called Zaro and Jiro who were part of a pack of fifteen huskies sent to the South Pole as sled dogs for two Japanese expeditions in 1956 and 1958.

At the end of the expeditions, the base was

Mountain Survivor's Tip

A sled with a heavy weight on it can pick up momentum going downhill. It is incredibly hard to slow down or turn, so always try to keep your sled under control but make sure you can jump clear of the harness if necessary.

closed and the dogs were left in Antarctica over the winter with virtually no chance of survival. However, the following year, in 1959, some of the members of the previous expedition returned and were astounded to find that two of the dogs had survived. Zaro and Jiro recognized the men and rushed to greet them. They were flown back to Hokkaido in Japan, where they received a heroes' welcome.

MOUNTAIN SURVIVAL STORIES

MOUNTAIN SURVIVAL STORIES

So, that got some of the theory out of the way . . . but don't forget, I'll be checking up at the end of the book to make sure you were paying attention. For now, though, let's get down to hearing about some remarkable and exemplary stories of real-life mountain survival.

All of the following survivors have exhibited enormous reserves of indomitable spirit, and it's worth remembering that anyone can be a victim, but could we all be survivors? How do you think you might have done in similar circumstances?

INTO THE ABYSS

In June 1985, three British ice climbers set off on a trip to South America. One day Joe Simpson and his pal Simon Yates set out to climb Siula Grande, a 21,000-ft (6,401-m) mountain in the Peruvian Andes. The friends reached the summit and then started to make their way down. During their descent, a bad snowstorm closed in and they drifted off course. Eventually, the tired climbers reached a sheer ice cliff and neither of them knew just how far down it went. The pair decided they would have to try to get down, so they tied Joe Simpson to a rope and Simon Yates lowered him over the edge.

NO RETURN

Unfortunately, once Simon had let out all the rope, Joe still hadn't reached the bottom. Simon tried to hoist Joe back up, but after an hour of trying, the dead weight of his friend was starting to pull Simon over the edge. Finally, Simon decided that he had no other option left to him — if he continued they would both die — so he cut the rope and Joe dropped.

MIRACULOUS ESCAPE

With a heavy heart Simon Yates then worked his way down the cliff and around the mountain until he reached base. Unbeknownst to him, Joe had fallen and fallen into the void but, remarkably, he had landed on a large ledge inside a crevasse. He stayed there for two days, passing in and out of consciousness because he had sustained terrible injuries — two broken legs, broken ribs, and a broken ankle. However, on the third day, he managed to crawl out and drag himself down the mountain. Could you have overcome the pain of your injuries to achieve such a feat?

Eventually, he got to within a few hundred yards of the base camp and collapsed. Simon Yates, his fellow climber Richard, and the porters were just packing up and preparing to leave, having given up the rescue search, when they heard Joe's shouting, swearing, and screaming.

They could not believe he was still alive. There were a few awkward moments between Joe and Simon, particularly when Joe found out that Simon had burned all his clothes. Joe asked him, "Why?" and Simon replied, "I thought you were . . ." but he couldn't finish the sentence. It was obvious that no one thought Joe was coming back and this unspoken truth released the tension between the two old friends and they ended up laughing uncontrollably.

Simon then helped carry Joe down the mountain, sharing a tent with him so he could tend his wounds, and Joe eventually made a full recovery.

It must have taken supreme efforts and enormous will for Joe to pull himself out of the crevasse and down the mountain. This story also illustrates the unparalleled strength of the bonds of friendship. Could you have brought yourself to cut that rope? Or, harder still, could you forgive the friend who let you drop? Both impossibly hard decisions for friends to make!

Mountain Survivor's Tip

Don't put your head inside your sleeping bag in freezing weather because your breath condenses and makes you cold. Wear a balaclava and keep your head out of the bag!

STORM OF THE CENTURY

In the spring of 1993, the United States was hit by a massive storm. It deluged enough water to submerge much of New York State. Of course, the ensuing floods and hurricane devastation were bad enough, but for the unsuspecting few caught in the hills, this storm brought disastrous blizzards.

Teenager Danielle Swank was on a school trip to the Appalachian Mountains. She and her school friends were all taken by surprise by the ferocity of the blizzard that hit them. The group tried to stick together to find their way out of the blizzard but Danielle and her teacher, Mr. Woodruff, were finding the going tough. They started to lag behind and eventually became separated from the main group on the eighth day of their ordeal.

Mr. Woodruff was suffering considerably and Danielle tried to make him as comfortable as possible, but she, too, was suffering the effects of exposure. On the ninth night, Danielle's feet were so painful that she took off her boots and left them outside her makeshift shelter. The next morning her feet had swollen and her boots were frozen, so she couldn't get them back on. By now, their spirits were at an all-time low. Little did they know, but the biggest peacetime search-and-rescue effort in U.S. history was being played out over 1,640 sq ft (500 sq m) of backcountry in an attempt to find survivors.

LUCKY ESCAPE

Mr. Woodruff could go no further but Danielle tried to continue with little success. She thought they were doomed. However, later that day, a rescue helicopter spotted Danielle and picked her up. She was given emergency first aid for her hypothermia and flown directly to the hospital where some of the toes on her right foot had to be amputated. Danielle described Mr. Woodruff's location and condition and he, too, was brought to the hospital, but when the rescuers found him, his feet were literally complete blocks of ice.

Danielle showed great courage during her ordeal and she was one of the lucky ones who survived. Two hundred and seventy people lost their lives to "the storm of the century." Those who remained close to their camps, cabins, or cars tended to be rescued fairly quickly, but for those caught in the open, such as Danielle and her fellow students, help was a long time in coming, and for the unfortunate few, it came too late.

What if . . . you found yourself stranded high in the mountains with an injured or unconscious friend? Would you try to carry them out or might there be another alternative?

In general, it's recommended that a casualty should be left where they are until help can arrive. However, if no one knows you're missing and no rescue is likely, you need to get yourself and your casualty down into the valleys as soon as possible, where food and shelter are available.

The best way to transport heavy loads or someone who cannot walk by themselves is by using a sled, also known as a pulk, that you can pull across the ice and snow.

MAKING A SLED

❄ Find a strong, forked tree branch. Then tie the ends of the branches to the main part of the bough to tension the curves.

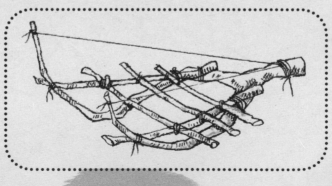

❄ Brace the bottom runners for additional strength by lashing sticks across the curve. These also form the support for the seat.

❄ Lash sticks between the two bracing struts to form the main platform/seat of the sled. The more crosspieces possible, the more secure the platform.

❄ A pulling handle can then be made from a branch that goes across the chest and two pieces of cord that attach it securely to the sled.

❄ The casualty and equipment (tied on) can then be put on the sled and, presto, you're off!

ANTARCTIC AGONIES

At the beginning of the last century, explorers turned their attention to the unexplored expanses of Antarctica.

Amundsen was the first to reach the South Pole on December 14, 1911, closely followed by Scott, who died in the attempt, on January 16, 1912.

An Australian geologist named Douglas Mawson had visited Antarctica on Shackleton's 1907 to 1909 expedition, and in 1911 he decided to return leading his own party. His was the first Antarctic expedition to use a new and modern piece of technology — the radio! But there was only one on the ship and one at the main base on Commonwealth Bay.

The expedition carried out a good deal of research in the area and it was on one such excursion that disaster struck.

CREVASSE CRISIS

A three-man sledding party set out to explore the area to the east of their base. Mawson, the expedition leader, was accompanied by Mertz, a Swiss ski champion, and Ninnis, a British officer.

On December 14, 1912, the party came across a crevasse. Mertz carefully crossed a snowbridge spanning the crevasse, followed by Mawson. However, when they looked around for their companion, there was no one to be seen on the white landscape behind them. Ninnis, his dogs, and his sled had all completely disappeared.

Horrified, Mawson and Mertz realized that the fragile snowbridge they had just crossed must have collapsed together with their companion. They rushed back and peered over the edge, praying, hope against hope, that he would be on a ledge just below the surface, suspended by his harness, but there was nothing to be seen. About 40 yd (36.5 m) down, an injured dog lay whimpering on an icy ledge but despite their urgent calls, no reply came from Ninnis. The crevasse was so deep that they could not even see the bottom.

DOUBLE TRAGEDY

The two disbelieving friends stayed for over three hours at the edge of the crevasse, calling and hoping for some sign of life, but eventually they had to admit the terrible truth — Ninnis would never return from his icy tomb.

Tragically, Ninnis's sled had been equipped with the best dogs and was carrying the party's tent, all the dogs' food, and most of the men's supplies. Just how low would you feel having lost a friend and then making this discovery?

The two pressed on because they knew they were 300 mi (483 km) from their base with no tent and only a ten-day supply of food, despite the fact that it had taken them five weeks to get there.

EXTREME SURVIVAL

The pair made a makeshift shelter from a spare tent cover and Mertz's skis, and they eked out their meager supplies by boiling the empty food bags to make thin soup. The hungry dogs were fed gloves, old boots, and leather straps to keep them from starving.

In desperation, they killed and ate the remaining six dogs. They found the livers the easiest to eat raw but little did they know that eating animal livers can kill you! Soon after, Mertz started behaving strangely — at one point, he bit off his own frostbitten finger — until he eventually died after a sudden fit (probably due to vitamin A poisoning from eating the livers).

ALONE IN THE ANTARCTIC

By now, Mawson must have felt desperate. He had lost his two companions and was all alone still 100 mi (161 km) from base. Yet Mawson was determined to make it back. By now, his hair was coming out in clumps, he had frostbite in his toes and fingers, and the only thing keeping the skin on the bottom of his feet were the bandages and six pairs of socks he'd put on!

Slowly he set off, dragging his sled himself. To make his task easier, he sawed the sled in half down the middle using a penknife to make it lighter.

A NARROW ESCAPE

During his epic journey, Mawson too fell into a crevasse and he must have thought he was going to suffer the same horrendous fate as Ninnis. However, his sled got jammed at the top of the crevasse and the harness held Mawson dangling above the void. If the sled had come tumbling down on top of him, he'd have been finished, but it didn't. He managed to drag himself up the 10-ft (3-m) rope harness and to scramble free of the hole. What a terrifying experience, eh?

There were many occasions when Mawson could have given up. He'd been traveling three weeks on his own when, 30 mi (48 km) from the base, he stumbled across a food dump, which probably saved his life.

Saved from the brink of starvation, Mawson dug deep and found the necessary energy to drag himself the final distance to the hut.

THE FINAL BLOW

On February 1, 1913, he dragged himself over the final hill that shielded his base. To his utter amazement and despair, he saw that his expedition ship, the *Aurora*, was sailing away without him! After all he'd been through, this was probably the worst moment of his life.

Luckily, and unbeknownst to him, although the *Aurora* was sailing away to avoid the winter ice, a team of six men had been left behind in case the Mawson party made it back. Mawson crawled into the hut with a heavy heart where he, at last, found help. However, he had lost so much weight during his ordeal — he weighed half his original weight — that his rescuers didn't know which member of the original party he was.

Mawson retold his remarkable story and the ship was recalled using the new radio equipment. However, severe gales prevented the ship's return and so Mawson and his six companions were forced to spend the winter at base camp. They were picked up the following spring but Mawson would never forget his horrendous ordeal — or the friends he'd lost.

It was always Mawson's belief that the only reason he did not suffer the same fate as Ninnis was that he was sitting on his sled, which spread his weight as he crossed the narrow bridge, whereas Ninnis walked alongside his sled, which concentrated his weight. We'll never know for sure, but it was definitely a narrow escape.

Fact File
A crevasse is created when the ice splits apart as it slowly moves over hidden rocks far below. The crevasse is often concealed with snow so you don't know it's there until it's too late.

Fact File

Crevasses tend to be extremely deep but can vary from as little as a few inches to as much as 100 feet or more across.

One of the biggest problems for Antarctic explorers is that a crevasse can open up unexpectedly right in their path. This, combined with extreme temperatures and the strongest winds on earth, known as katabatic winds, which can rip a tent to shreds in seconds, is what makes exploration in the Antarctic such a risky business.

Mountain Survivor's Tip

To prevent snow blindness, use whatever is at hand to make a pair of slit goggles. Some resourceful survivors have found that the cardboard cover of a map will suffice, and even the film out of a camera has been used to good effect.

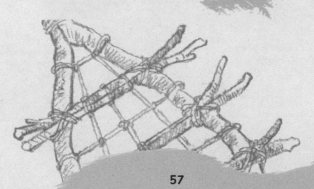

AVALANCHE ADVENTURES

AVALANCHE ADVENTURES

When you think of dangers in the mountains, the first thing to spring to mind is probably an avalanche. And with just cause. Avalanches have claimed the lives of numerous climbers, skiers, and walkers from every level of experience, and even whole communities. In fact, in the winter of 2000, twelve people died when an airborne blast of snow smashed twenty chalets in the ski resort of Argentiere in the French Alps. Then, within days, another thirty-one were killed when an even bigger avalanche engulfed the Austrian ski village of Galtur.

Avalanche prediction is a science that the experts are still perfecting but, as a result of painstaking research, it is now less common for populated areas to be wiped out because we no longer build in known avalanche paths and because we have better knowledge for building avalanche defenses.

Nonetheless, the "White Death," as avalanches were known in the past, still poses a threat to the unwary adventurer, as this selection of avalanche survival stories from a relatively small area of the Highlands of Scotland will attest.

TROUBLE IN THE CAIRNGORMS

On December 28, 1964, a group of young men set off to climb Beinn a'Bhuird, which, at 3,924 ft (1,196 m), is one of the six highest Cairngorm peaks. As a scoutmaster, Alexander MacKenzie was trying to complete his Rambler's Badge and his friends Alasdair Murray, Robert Burnett, and Alexander McLeod, all experienced hill-walkers, had agreed to go along with him.

After a good ascent, they descended from the top of the mountain toward a sheltered campsite by the creek where they intended to spend the second night of their trip. Robert Burnett tested the snow as they descended and found it firm. Alasdair Murray, who was leading the party, slipped and fell into the gully but, as he was unhurt, got up and continued down the creek, intending to meet up with his friends at the bottom.

CHAPTER FIVE

DISASTER STRIKES

All of a sudden, the snow broke away below Burnett's feet, carrying him down the mountain. The last thing he remembered was waving his hands above his head to attract attention. This single act may well have saved his life, because when he regained consciousness, he was on his back under the snow with his hands above his head. Luckily for him, he was able to move his arms and scrape the snow off his face so he could breathe from a little air pocket.

However, Burnett was held solid in his icy tomb and he began frantically calling for help. Meanwhile, unbeknownst to him, two others of the party had also been swept away. Alasdair Murray was unscathed as he witnessed his friends' disappearance beneath the avalanche. He desperately started to search for them using a stick to probe the deep snow.

After a fruitless half hour, he decided to give up and go for help. Murray ran for 5 mi (8 km) to the nearest human help. A rescue party was quickly formed and they made their way into the hills to the scene of the accident.

GRUESOME DISCOVERY

During the night, they discovered the body of Alexander McLeod, but the search continued. In the early hours of the morning the search was called off but, despite feelings of grave misgivings, the search resumed in the morning, when thirty soldiers joined the rescue attempt.

After some hours, a rescuer noticed a small hole in the debris that was yellowed around the edges. He peered into the hole, and to his amazement, he saw Burnett, not only alive but calling for help.

Hastily, he was dug out from the snow that was covering him. He was suffering from frostbite, which was hardly surprising considering he'd been buried for some twenty-two hours! He was rushed to the hospital and made a full recovery from his injuries. Sadly, Alexander MacKenzie, the final member of the party, was not so lucky — he was found dead some hours later.

Fact File
Statistics show that only
3 percent of people survive
a burial by avalanche for
more than two hours.

CHAPTER FIVE

Mountain Survivor's Tip

Caught in an Avalanche
If you found yourself caught in an avalanche,
would you know what to do?
Hopefully, you'd be able to keep a cool-
enough head to remember these
lifesaving techniques.

❄ Shout out to draw the attention of others to your plight.

❄ Discard your equipment such as ice ax, backpack, ski poles, etc.

❄ Attempt to stay on the surface of the snow using a freestyle or backstroke swimming action.

❄ Try to escape to the side of the fall by rolling sideways like a log or by using the swimming action.

❄ If still caught in the snow as the avalanche stops, use all your energy to thrust your hand, foot, or body to the surface.

❄ If buried, try to create a breathing space around your face as the avalanche slows.

❄ Once all movement has stopped, try to conserve energy by staying relaxed and only shout if you hear rescuers and you're likely to be heard.

INGENUITY REIGNS

Two hill-walkers were buried under 8 ft (2.4 m) of blocklike snow in the northern Cairngorms on January 11, 1997. With both knocked unconscious, they had only the slimmest chance of survival. But as one came around, he became aware that, although trapped, he could breathe. Cracks had opened in the avalanche debris and, luckily for him, his face was in one of them. He could hear their dog barking and, more amazing still, when he called out, he heard his friend reply from some distance away within their tomb.

GRIM DETERMINATION

Although his body was stuck, the man could move his head, and gradually, over several hours, he was able to nod out enough space to free his right hand. Luckily, this was just above the left breast pocket of his jacket, containing his compass. Using all his resourcefulness, the man started to use the tiny compass as a makeshift shovel with which he painstakingly dug himself, and subsequently his companion, out of the snow.

The self-reliant pair reached the parking lot at the Cairngorm ski area just as the rescue team was setting out.

Now that's what I call resourceful!

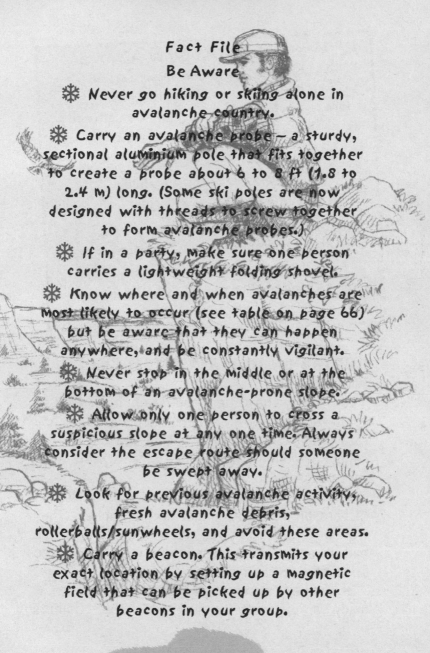

Fact File
Be Aware

❄ Never go hiking or skiing alone in avalanche country.

❄ Carry an avalanche probe — a sturdy, sectional aluminium pole that fits together to create a probe about 6 to 8 ft (1.8 to 2.4 m) long. (Some ski poles are now designed with threads to screw together to form avalanche probes.)

❄ If in a party, make sure one person carries a lightweight folding shovel.

❄ Know where and when avalanches are most likely to occur (see table on page 66) but be aware that they can happen anywhere, and be constantly vigilant.

❄ Never stop in the middle or at the bottom of an avalanche-prone slope.

❄ Allow only one person to cross a suspicious slope at any one time. Always consider the escape route should someone be swept away.

❄ Look for previous avalanche activity, fresh avalanche debris, rollerballs/sunwheels, and avoid these areas.

❄ Carry a beacon. This transmits your exact location by setting up a magnetic field that can be picked up by other beacons in your group.

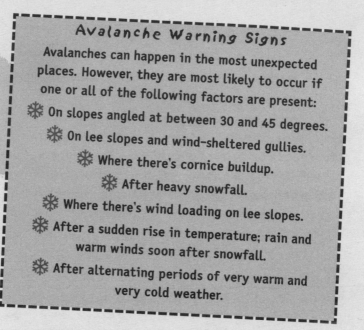

Avalanche Warning Signs

Avalanches can happen in the most unexpected places. However, they are most likely to occur if one or all of the following factors are present:

❄ On slopes angled at between 30 and 45 degrees.

❄ On lee slopes and wind-sheltered gullies.

❄ Where there's cornice buildup.

❄ After heavy snowfall.

❄ Where there's wind loading on lee slopes.

❄ After a sudden rise in temperature; rain and warm winds soon after snowfall.

❄ After alternating periods of very warm and very cold weather.

BURIED ON BRITAIN'S TALLEST MOUNTAIN

Ben Nevis, the tallest mountain in Britain at 4,409 ft (1,344 m), has witnessed many tragic and fatal avalanche accidents but, on April 1, 1967, a couple of young climbers had a remarkable April Fool's escape.

Andrew Philipson and his cousin David Richardson were both experienced climbers. They were both well equipped and well dressed for the bad weather conditions they were about to encounter on the mountain.

It was very gusty and cold, and the new snow made it difficult to navigate. The climbers realized they were off course, and started to traverse across the slope to get back on track. At about two PM, a huge avalanche swept the men about 525 ft (160 m) down the mountain and left them both buried.

DIRE SITUATION

Things could not have been worse: No one saw them fall and they were off course. The one glimmer of hope was that both men were able to breathe and they were well insulated against the snow that encased them.

Philipson was entombed about 4 feet (1.2 m) below the surface, which would normally mean certain death. However, he showed remarkable determination and fortitude and, after nine hours of scraping and scratching at the snow with his hands, he managed to struggle into the night air. He then staggered down the mountain to a hut where, fortunately, some Oxford climbers were staying.

TO THE RESCUE

After phoning the police, the Oxford climbers hastily assembled a rescue party and set off to search for Richardson. They retraced Philipson's tracks up the mountain to the scene of the avalanche and, without much hope, set about searching for the missing man. After eleven hours, each of them believed he was looking for a corpse.

So, imagine their surprise and delight when, soon after midnight, a searcher saw a hand sticking out from the snow. Everyone started furiously digging to reveal that Richardson was not only alive, but conscious. A remarkable escape and double miracle!

Mountain Survivor's Tip

Search for avalanche victims by trees and benches first — this is the place where people are most commonly buried.

Fact File

How to Search for an Avalanche
Victim

If you see someone taken by an avalanche:

❆ Check for further danger before and
while searching.

❆ Mark the spot where you last saw
him/her before he/she went under, and then
the place where the avalanche hit the person.
Draw an imaginary line through these two
points and continue it below to find the
most likely place of burial.

❆ Call for help, but don't leave the area
to find assistance that is more than
fifteen minutes away.

❆ Look for anything like personal items that
may indicate where the burial site is.

❆ Systematically check the area by
probing with an avalanche probe or, if not,
with an ax shaft, ski pole, or some
improvised probe.

❆ On finding the victim, clear the mouth
and airways of snow. Remove the weight of
snow from the chest. Give artificial
respiration immediately if the person is not
breathing, even before fully removing
the body from the snow.

MOUNTAIN RESCUES

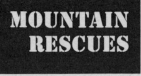

MOUNTAIN RESCUES

Despite all the laws of survival that dictate that you never put yourself at risk to save another, this is precisely what mountain rescue teams do on a regular basis. These brave individuals are proof that acts of selflessness still occur in our rather cynical, selfish, modern world, and this is heartening.

The teams are made up of experienced mountain men and women who volunteer to search for and rescue those in peril in the mountains. Every time they are called out, they potentially endanger their own lives.

Of course, they are well equipped with the latest gear and technology now, but in the early days of mountain rescue this was not quite the case. There's a story about Sid Cross, who was one of the first team leaders with the Langdale Mountain Rescue team in the Lake District in Britain in the early 1950s. In those days, they had no radios and very few members. So if there was an emergency, Sid would dive into the local pub and grab a few likely-looking volunteers for the team.

Without radio communications with his teams in the hills, Sid came up with an ingenious solution. He acquired a small cannon and he'd send off a shell blast into the sky to recall people when a rescue was completed. Eccentric, maybe, but it worked. What would you have done to get the message through?

Anybody who has benefited from the reassuring and comforting presence of the mountain rescue volunteers will undoubtedly have the utmost respect for their work. Here you can judge for yourselves as you get just a small taste of some of their heroic exploits.

INJURED AND ALONE

On the evening of April 3, 2000, the Riverside Mountain Rescue Unit (RMRU) in California was called out to

Humber Park to rescue a fallen hiker. Ten members responded to the call. After a short briefing, a hasty two-person team was sent to the site with medical gear.

David Carrick, an eighteen-year-old from a private high school in Fresno, had tripped while hiking on the north side of Tahquitz Rock. This area is known to be very hazardous due to its very steep slopes covered in loose rocks. David was part of a group of other seniors taking part in a senior weekend party.

They came to Humber Park to do a little hiking around. However, when they got to Humber Park they all went off in various directions from the school vans that brought them. Some had gone as groups, others, apparently, by themselves. David was one of those who ventured off alone.

FALLING HEADLONG

While hiking up at the base of Tahquitz, he slipped and fell an unknown distance, landing facedown in some rocks. While falling he both heard and felt his neck crack. He was very smart at this point and thought that he should not move his body until help arrived. Fortunately for him, one of the counselors with the group just happened upon him by chance. He then sent some of the other boys down to get help while he stayed with David.

When the RMRU team arrived on site they did an in-depth medical examination of David, while a second team was en route with a special litter that has a big wheel under it. Even before the second team arrived on the scene, a third team was sent up from base to assist.

David was stabilized into the litter and they began the hard, slow descent back down to base camp. David had to be belayed with ropes all the way back to base camp. After two and a half hours, the seven-person RMRU team got David back to camp and into the waiting ambulance.

A LONG NIGHT

After a debriefing, the RMRU members hurried home at four AM to try to get a couple hours of sleep before starting their normal jobs in the morning as if nothing had happened.

David was transported to Loma Linda Hospital where it was later found that he had a broken upper jaw and had fractured two vertebrae in his spine.

The lesson to be learned here is always hike with at least one other person. Had the counselor not come across David by chance, RMRU would have had several square miles to search for him once he did not show up at the vans. They would not even have been able to track him due to the terrain. This could have been a long and difficult search for a severely injured missing person.

Fact File
The RMRU is an all-volunteer search-and-rescue team that covers Riverside County and assists other teams with search-and-rescue efforts in other counties. Each member purchases his/her own equipment and takes time off from work, without compensation, to participate in search-and-rescue missions. Team equipment is purchased from contributions from the community. It is a nonprofit organization and is funded by donations from the public. For further details, check out www.rmru.org.

Mountain Survivor's Tip

You must never move a casualty if you suspect a spinal injury. If the person has a neck fracture, like David Carrick, the neck should be immobilized with a cervical collar. In the mountains, it's unlikely that you'll have such a collar. So, if the casualty is on his/her back, place a rolled towel or cloth under the neck to support it and place two weighted objects (a pair of weighted boots will do) on either side of the head to keep it stable and stationary until help arrives.

TROUBLE ON NEVIS

February 19, 1994, proved to be the busiest day ever for the Lochaber Mountain Rescue Team since it had begun. Conditions were appalling on Britain's tallest mountain, but thirty-five-year-old Richard from London and his female companion had reached the summit of 4,400-ft (1,341-m) Ben Nevis from the north face and were starting their descent when disaster struck.

In the whiteout storm, the pair needed to navigate across a narrow plateau with steep cliffs on either side. Unfortunately, Richard lost his footing and fell 800 ft (244 m) into the 3,000-

ft (914-m) Five Finger Gulley. His crampons caught and his body whiplashed over, causing a compound leg fracture as he tumbled on. His colleague desperately tried to make her way down to where he lay, at the same time sending a distress signal with her flashlight. Could you have been this levelheaded in a crisis?

GALE-FORCE WINDS

The signal was picked up and a helicopter was called. But the pilot radioed that the gale-force winds coming over the top of the ridge would not allow him into the gulley. The rescue would have to be done by volunteers on the ground!

To move Richard to where the chopper could pick him up involved negotiating him on a stretcher down a 2,000-ft (610-m) drop. The rescuers needed to traverse down 8,000 ft (2,438 m) to reach him. Then, in four stages and on 500-ft (152-m) ropes, they had to lower him to the floor of the gulley.

DANGEROUS DESCENT

In the pitch-dark, Richard was lashed to the stretcher and, together with a team member with a radio at his neck to give instructions, they were lowered down. It took more than three hours to get him down the cliff.

The RAF Rescue helicopter flew Richard to a hospital at Inverness where his horrific injuries — ice burns to the face, severe cuts to his fingers and arms, his foot hanging from a

Pott's fracture — were patched up. Thankfully, he made a full recovery.

Meanwhile, the Lochabar Mountain Rescue Team was back on the mountain helping a woman who had been stranded on Cairngorm for forty-one hours. During the course of that fateful day and night in February, they were called on to deal with ten incidents — two of them fatal — and it was four AM before the exhausted team eventually got to bed.

Fact File
A whiteout is where snow and dense mist mingle to reduce visibility to less than a few feet.

DARK CANYON RESCUE

On December 17, 2000, the RMRU was called out to search for twenty-four-year-old Frederico Chaves, Jr., who was reported missing by his friend Jason Vega. The pair had hiked the Marion Mountain Trail to San Jacinto Peak starting out at eight-thirty AM, reaching the peak at about three PM.

Wanting to hike at different speeds, Jason and Fred separated near Little Round Valley. Jason reached their vehicle at about five-thirty PM but Fred was nowhere to be found.

GETTING WORRIED

Jason honked the horn of the vehicle and yelled for his friend but there was no response. Finding a pay phone, Jason tried to call Fred's cell phone but nobody answered. Jason then contacted authorities who alerted RMRU.

The first search team from RMRU started up the Marion Mountain Trail by ten PM and the second team was dispatched to the Seven Pines Trail an hour later. Teams searched throughout the night on the steep and icy trails. Due to the urgency of the situation, Desert Sheriff Search and Rescue (DSSAR) from Palm Desert was contacted for additional personnel and a helicopter was scheduled for seven-thirty AM.

Shortly after four AM, a mixed RMRU/DSSAR Team started up the Deer Springs Trail with an RMRU Team heading down. A second DSSAR member was held in reserve to act as an aerial observer when the helicopter arrived but was used as a radio relay instead.

Fact File

It's not just humans who have an overwhelming desire to help others in distress. In 1975, Mark Cooper left his home in California on a trip to the Sierra Nevada with his faithful dog, Zorro, a German shepherd. Unfortunately, while walking in the mountains, Mark lost his balance and toppled into a ravine, falling 85 ft. He was knocked out and landed in a stream below.

When he came to, he realized that Zorro was trying to pull him out of the freezing water and up a steep rocky slope. Mark was later found by friends who went to get help while Zorro lay on top of him and kept him warm.

The next day, a helicopter was brought in and Mark was winched to safety, but, in the hubbub, Zorro was left behind. Days later he was spotted by walkers, guarding Mark's backpack in a touching display of loyalty. He was later honored with the American Dog Hero of the Year Award. What a cool dog!

FOUND ALIVE

At 7:12 AM, Team 1 established voice contact with Fred and within a few minutes made physical contact with him in a ravine approximately a half mile off the trail.

Reaching the Marion Mountain Trail and Pacific Crest/Deer Springs Trail intersection, Fred had made a common mistake and turned south instead of continuing west on the Marion Mountain Trail. Not realizing his mistake, he continued several miles down Deer Springs Trail until he became lost.

Fred then decided to go straight down the mountain and "headed for the lights" of the town. However, after falling several times, he wisely decided to stop for the night. Fred had a lighter and he lit a fire to melt snow and for warmth. He was reasonably warm, dressed in a fleece jacket and long pants.

Fred had a narrow escape. How do you think you would have coped with being alone and cold in the mountains for the night?

Mountain Survivor's Tip

If your party is caught in a blizzard and you're forced to shelter in several snow holes, make sure you put a rope between them so you can find one another if you venture into the storm. People have been known to get lost just trying to reach the neighboring snow hole in a whiteout blizzard. Push sticks/ski poles up through the roof of your snow hole to mark the spot so no one crashes through your roof when stumbling around outside.

A CAUTIONARY TALE

Members of a mountain rescue team were somewhat puzzled when they were called to the aid of a young girl who kept collapsing at the top of Cader Idris, a 2,700-ft (823-m) mountain in Wales. She and her party took shelter in the hut at the top of the mountain until the rescue team could get to her. The experienced first-aiders in the team wondered if hypothermia was causing the blackouts, but she didn't exhibit any of the normal symptoms. She was subsequently taken down the mountain on a stretcher and transported to the nearest hospital.

Less than an hour later, the blushing girl was discharged. Apparently, she had been so embarrassed about having to relieve herself in the open air while camping out with her party of friends that she had not been to the toilet for three days. This had caused a kidney infection and that was why she kept blacking out. Of course, the poor girl was very embarrassed, but when the doctors told the rescue team, they all had a good laugh!

Mountain Survivor's Tip

We all have to go sometimes and if you're spending a few days in the great outdoors, be sensible about where you relieve yourself. It's best to urinate behind bushes, etc., to save any embarrassment, but if you need to do something more serious, then most outdoor types carry a small trowel so they can bury the evidence after they've performed. This is both environmentally sound and more pleasant for other walkers who might subsequently pass that way.

SAVING
LIVES

SAVING LIVES

You might be forgiven for thinking that the biggest danger to a person's health when stranded on a mountain is falling down a gully or breaking a leg. But the single most common threat to life comes from the environment itself — yes, hypothermia — when the body temperature drops below normal. It is the biggest killer in these high and exposed regions.

If you are in a group, it's up to you to look out for one another — that's what friends are for. Check that none of your friends is showing any signs of cold-climate ailments such as hypothermia or frostbite and be confident that they are doing the same for you.

Of course, things like twisted ankles or broken bones are quite common in the hills and a bit of basic first-aid knowledge could mean that you bring your party out of the mountains alive. . . . So read on, because, who knows? One day your friends' lives may depend on it.

HYPOTHERMIA

Freezing conditions mean that your body cannot generate heat as fast as it loses it and your temperature drops below normal.

SYMPTOMS

Shivering and goose bumps; apathy and confusion; inability to respond to questions; lack of coordination; lethargy interspersed with bursts of frenetic activity; lapses of consciousness; slow, shallow breathing; and a weak pulse.

TREATMENT

❄ The casualty must be rewarmed gradually.

❄ Prevent further heat loss by sheltering from the wind and weather and replacing wet clothing with dry. Don't strip off completely but replace a garment at a time.

❄ Give the patient warm fluids and sugary foods (only if conscious).

❄ One of the best ways to warm the patient is to strip them to their undergarments and get them into a sleeping bag with someone else who is warm and semi-naked — never mind your blushes, this is life and death!

❄ If not, apply warm rocks or a warm hot-water bottle to strategic areas of the body where blood supply is near the surface and so is able to carry heat through the body, namely: stomach, small of back, armpits, back of neck, wrists, and between thighs; or wrap in a foil blanket.

❆ Never give alcohol to someone suffering from hypothermia — this aggravates the condition.

❆ Once the patient's temperature reaches normal, you're not out of the woods yet! Their body reserves have to be rebuilt until they can generate heat internally again. So be vigilant and keep administering hot drinks, etc.

Mountain Survivor's Tip

Wet clothing, high winds, an injury that immobilizes, inactivity, worry and mental stress, and extreme thinness are all aggravating factors in susceptibility to hypothermia, so be particularly vigilant in these circumstances.

Fact File

An old Indian trick is to try to touch your little finger to your thumb. If you can't, you know you're in trouble because your hands are too cold to do simple tasks. Take remedial action.

FROSTBITE

This condition occurs when the skin and flesh freeze at temperatures below 30°F (−1°C). It usually affects the extremities with poorest circulation, i.e., feet, hands, nose, ears, and face.

SYMPTOMS

First signs are often a prickling sensation as the skin freezes. The affected areas then become waxy-looking and numb to the touch. Later, these patches become hard and bumpy with swelling, reddening, and blistering accompanied by considerable pain. In extreme cases, these areas eventually darken and become black, finally dying and dropping off.

TREATMENT

❄ Early frostbite that only affects the skin is known as frostnip. Treat this by placing the affected part in a warm area of your body. For example, put your hands under your armpits or in your groin. Put your feet against a friend's stomach (this is a real test of friendship!) and expect pain as the area thaws out.

❄ By the next stage, greater care is required. Thaw the area gradually with warm water at approximately 108°F (42°C) — about the temperature of a baby's bath, which is pleasantly warm when tested with your elbow.

❄ Advanced frostbite is best left to the experts. However, in emergencies, never rub the affected area or burst the blisters. Use your body warmth to warm.

Mountain Survivor's Tip

If you find yourself in extreme cold conditions, windmill your arms so the centrifugal force pushes blood down to your fingertips.

Fact File
Frostbite is a particular hazard of polar exploration. Sir Ranulph Fiennes, who undertook a solo walk from the U.S. to the North Pole in 2000, lost several fingers on his left hand due to frostbite after his arms and hands got wet in a sledding accident.

TRENCH FOOT

Long periods of exposure to cold and wet can cause numbing of the feet followed by swelling, making walking painful or impossible.

SYMPTOMS

A sensation of pins and needles or numbness, sharp pains, purple swelling, and blisters.

TREATMENT

❄ **Dry feet thoroughly.**

❄ **Do NOT massage or rub feet.**

❄ **Do NOT apply artificial heat.**

❄ **Elevate feet and cover to keep warm.**

Mountain Survivor's Tip

Prevent trench foot from developing by keeping feet dry, changing socks regularly, wearing well-fitting boots, and by inspecting your feet regularly.

SNOW BLINDNESS

A temporary form of blindness caused by the intense glare of the sun, which is reflected off the snow or intensified by the ice.

SYMPTOMS

Sensitivity to glare; blinking and squinting; vision takes on a pinkish hue, which becomes redder; gritty eyes; loss of vision; sharp pain.

TREATMENT

❄ **If possible, get into the dark and bandage eyes.**

❄ **Apply soothing cool, wet bandages to eyes or forehead.**

❄ **Allow time for eyes to recover.**

Mountain Survivor's Tip

Snow blindness is a very painful condition, which is best prevented. If possible, wear sunglasses or goggles. If not available, improvise with eyeshades by cutting slits in bark or some other blindfold. Darken the area around the eyes using charcoal to reduce the glare.

DEHYDRATION

Despite the cold, if you sweat through exertion and do not drink very much, the body will become dehydrated, i.e., lacking in water.

SYMPTOMS

Dark yellow, pungent urine and a headache.

TREATMENT

❄ Make sure you drink enough water even though you may not feel thirsty.

SPRAINED ANKLE
A wrenching or tearing of tissues connected with a joint.

SYMPTOMS
Pain, swelling, and later a bruise.

TREATMENT

❄ Bathe sprain with cold water to reduce swelling.

❄ Support with a bandage.

❄ Elevate foot and rest completely.

❄ If you have to keep walking on a sprained ankle, keep your boot on. If you take it off, the ankle will swell and prevent you from putting your boot back on. The boot acts like a splint if left on.

BROKEN BONES

If someone has a bad fall and breaks a bone, it will need setting once she or he gets to the hospital. In the meantime, you should try to support the affected part of the body above and below the break, perhaps using a makeshift splint or resting it on padding, and keep it steady in a comfortable position.

Mountain Survivor's Tip

Combat soldiers know that a casualty who is left to feel sorry for himself and alone for long periods will not make progress and may even die. Your responsibility is not only to administer first aid but also to keep the casualty's morale up and, injuries permitting, to give them minor tasks to occupy them and keep them distracted.

WHAT IF . . . ?

WHAT IF . . . ?

It's so easy, isn't it? We sit at home and watch these documentaries, quiz shows, and films, and it's always so obvious what the contestants are doing wrong. "No! You don't want to be under the bridge," you cry in exasperation at the TV, "you want to be at a vantage point!" Or whatever.

How could they be so dumb? you wonder. Well, that's easy. For a start, it's very much easier to make decisions when you're cool, calm, and collected and sitting comfortably in front of the television with a bowl of chips and a soda. It's harder when you're tired, uncomfortable, stressed, and hungry . . . all the conditions you might reasonably expect to find yourself in if you were in a real-life survival situation.

Nonetheless, it doesn't do any harm to give some thought to what you might do if you found yourself in the same situation . . . time invested in forethought and planning is never wasted, as my old commanding officer used to say.

So, why don't you get your thinking caps on and see what ideas you can come up with for the best course of action in the following perilous survival ordeals.

COUGAR ATTACK

You're out walking in the backcountry and you've strayed from your party. You find yourself alone in a rocky area of the mountain. Suddenly, you are aware of a snarling noise behind you. You turn around and are faced with a 6-ft (1.8-m) mountain lion about 10 ft (3 m) away. Although you can hear the voices of your friends, you have no idea how close they are. However, there is a small cluster of trees about 20 yd (18 m) ahead of you. What should you do?

MOUNTAIN SURVIVOR'S SOLUTIONS

Did you come up with something good? Feeling confident that you won't end up as a cougar snack? Well, let's see what the experts recommend.

You should bear in mind that there are no official studies telling us definitively what to do when faced with a mountain lion and that every situation is different. The following advice has been compiled from the stories of those who have come face-to-face with lions firsthand, and some patterns of lion behavior and response are beginning to emerge.

HOW TO ESCAPE FROM A MOUNTAIN LION

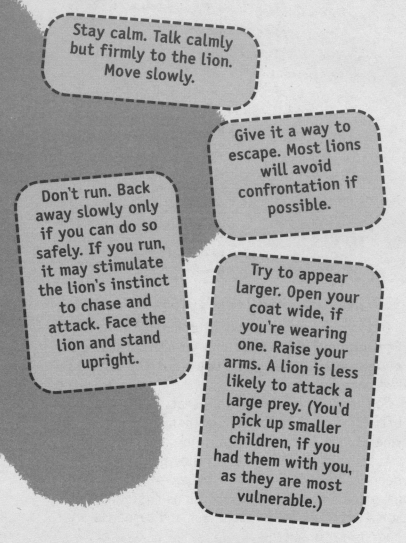

Stay calm. Talk calmly but firmly to the lion. Move slowly.

Give it a way to escape. Most lions will avoid confrontation if possible.

Don't run. Back away slowly only if you can do so safely. If you run, it may stimulate the lion's instinct to chase and attack. Face the lion and stand upright.

Try to appear larger. Open your coat wide, if you're wearing one. Raise your arms. A lion is less likely to attack a large prey. (You'd pick up smaller children, if you had them with you, as they are most vulnerable.)

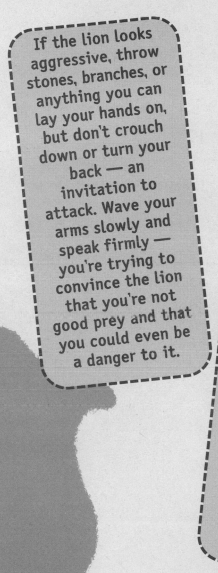

If the lion looks aggressive, throw stones, branches, or anything you can lay your hands on, but don't crouch down or turn your back — an invitation to attack. Wave your arms slowly and speak firmly — you're trying to convince the lion that you're not good prey and that you could even be a danger to it.

Fight back if a lion attacks you. People have reported successfully fighting back with rocks, sticks, caps, garden tools, and even their bare hands! Protect your neck and throat at all times to avoid the lion's "killing bite." Strike at its face, especially around the eyes and mouth. Never play dead — remain standing or try to get back up if knocked down.

So did you do the right thing? I hope you didn't head for the trees, a clue which I threw in as a bit of a red herring. Running would merely have triggered the cougar's instinct to chase its prey and, if you were lucky enough to reach the trees intact, lions are excellent climbers. So bad luck.

Fact File

Although cougar attacks remain rare in North America, they are increasing. In the 1990s, there were thirty-six recorded attacks, seven of which were fatal, compared with twenty including two fatal, in the 1980s; and seventeen, four of which were fatal in the 1970s. Sadly, in January 2001, a woman cross-country skier was stalked and killed by a cougar in the ski resort of Banff, Canada. The cougar had hidden behind a tree near the trail and pounced on Frances Frost, thirty, as she passed, killing her. The cat was later killed by park wardens.

Ian Syme, chief warden of the Banff National Park in the Rocky Mountains, said that cougars rarely attack human beings. However, he recommends that if you want to go skiing or hiking in the mountain wilderness, you should travel in a group and leave dogs at home because they attract cougars.

Other wildlife experts also add that you should make plenty of noise to reduce your chances of surprising a lion and carry a sturdy walking stick to ward off an attack. Make sure small children stay within sight and never approach a lion, especially if feeding or with kittens.

CASUALTY EVACUATION

You and your friends are on a climbing trip and you are many, many miles from the nearest populated area. One of your party falls, badly injuring himself. He is drifting in and out of consciousness. You use your cell phone to call for help. The rescue helicopter arrives but tells you that they cannot get close enough to your position to send down a winch because of the highly dangerous and unpredictable gusts of wind so close to the rock face. However, they can evacuate your injured friend if you can move the casualty half a mile down the mountain to an easier evacuation spot (they give you the map coordinates). You have no stretcher but you do have walking sticks, climbing rope, a tent, and camping equipment in your packs.

What's your plan for getting your pal to the helicopter pickup point for the help he so desperately needs?

MOUNTAIN SURVIVOR'S SOLUTIONS

Did you come up with any bright ideas? Hopefully, you decided to improvise with the equipment that you had in the packs. For those of you who thought you might be able to carry the casualty to the rendezvous point, just experiment with carrying someone without any equipment — one to one, two carrying one. How far would you get like this? Not far, and that's without a semiconscious casualty!

No, far and away the best bet is to improvise a stretcher. I'd love to see some of your ideas. . . . But here are a few of mine.

ROPE

Alpine coiled and used to help one person piggyback, or split between two people to carry a third who sits on the knot. Uncoiled and used to make a Roscoe Rope Stretcher.

TENT FLYSHEET

With sides rolled to make handles or wrapped around socks/pebbles with lashings to make handles.

POLES

Used with jackets. Zip up jackets with sleeves inside body with poles through sleeves.

Did you come up with any of those, or perhaps you had some even better ideas? You might also like to give consideration to some of the issues that an emergency situation such as this throws out. For example, who is in charge of route finding? How often do you rotate carriers? Are you having one voice in control? Who is going to carry the stretcher-bearers' and the casualty's packs and other equipment? Do you have a first-aid monitor? Isn't it amazing how many decisions you have to make on the spot when disaster strikes?

LIGHTNING STRIKES!

It's late afternoon and you and your pals are returning to camp in the high mountains after a great day's hiking. However, the weather is closing in and you find yourselves in open ground when a terrific thunderstorm breaks. Your camp is only ten minutes' walk but you have to cross an exposed mountain ridge to reach it. There are only a few isolated trees near you offering any shelter from the rain. Should you try and make it back to camp or stay where you are? Are you best seeking shelter under a tree or should you look elsewhere? It's your call.

MOUNTAIN SURVIVOR'S SOLUTIONS

So what did you decide? I hope to goodness you didn't cross that ridge — you'd be a sitting duck out there. Did you shelter under the tree? Well, brave the rain next time — isolated or small groups of trees act as ideal conductors for lightning strikes. Here are a few tips for next time you find yourself in a storm:

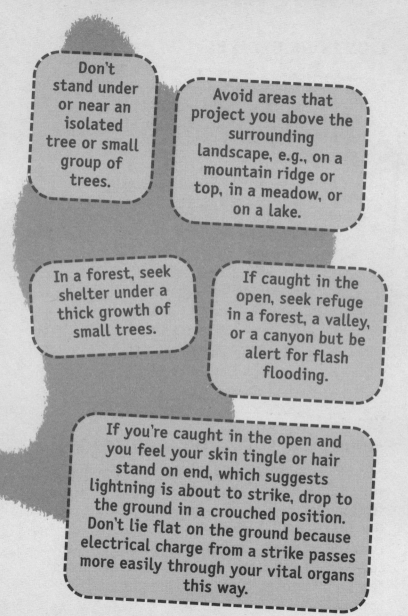

Don't stand under or near an isolated tree or small group of trees.

Avoid areas that project you above the surrounding landscape, e.g., on a mountain ridge or top, in a meadow, or on a lake.

In a forest, seek shelter under a thick growth of small trees.

If caught in the open, seek refuge in a forest, a valley, or a canyon but be alert for flash flooding.

If you're caught in the open and you feel your skin tingle or hair stand on end, which suggests lightning is about to strike, drop to the ground in a crouched position. Don't lie flat on the ground because electrical charge from a strike passes more easily through your vital organs this way.

Fact File
The electrical power produced by an "average" thunderstorm is around 250 million watts. To put that in perspective, it takes only 60 watts to light a table lamp and 400,000 to power a large supermarket. If the energy from a single lightning flash could be harnessed, it would supply power to several homes for a month!

Fact File

In Colorado, lightning is the number-one life-threatening weather hazard. In the last forty years, lightning has claimed the lives of more than 100 people in Colorado and has injured more than 300. Each year, in the U.S. as a whole, over 40 million lightning strikes occur in the contiguous states, killing nearly 100 people. Almost all of these casualties were engaged in outdoor activities, many in the mountains.

(Courtesy of The Colorado Mountain Club Federation)

MOUNTAIN SURVIVOR'S BRAIN-TEASERS

MOUNTAIN SURVIVOR'S BRAIN-TEASERS

If you're inspired by the stories in this book and you decide you'd like to learn a bit more about survival in the mountains, there are some excellent mountain craft and leadership courses run by outdoor education specialists, scouting associations, and volunteer organizations around the world. Most of them, at some point or another, will use training exercises to test your resourcefulness, team-building qualities, and your mountain knowledge. So, let's take a sneak preview and see how you do with this typical exercise, shall we?

SURVIVAL IN THE HILLS

A group of you has gotten yourselves into a mess. It is late October and you have set off on a hiking trip in the Sierra Nevada mountains of California. After catching a train, you hike into the mountains.

On the first day, you reached refuge at camp and on the second, you press deeper into the hills.

It is now the end of the third day and you have been stuck in your tent for twenty-four hours since it started to snow. The weather, up until the evening of the second day, had been mild, but a decrease in visibility was accompanied by a rapid drop in temperature.

Snow started to fall at about eight PM on that second evening and, with only short breaks, has continued to do so right up until now. You are worried since the position you camped in is far from ideal. The shortest route to the nearest help is by footpath and this means a trek through the snow of 6 to 7 mi (10 to 11 km).

Visibility is down to about 25 yd (23 m), and a northeasterly wind, force six, is blowing. The temperature is in the range of 27°F to 36°F (−3°C to 2°C). The snow is 2 ft (.6 m) deep all over, but drifting makes the conditions treacherous, especially since it is newly laid and walking is difficult in soft snow.

WHAT TO DO

You are faced with a series of choices. Regrettably, your group did not inform the police or rescue services of your route before setting out, and with the poor visibility, no one will find the tent in the foreseeable future. The weather shows no sign of improving and one of your group is beginning to suffer from hypothermia. It seems that your only chance of survival is to send one or more, or all, of your party to get help.

QUESTIONS

How many of you should go? What equipment should you take?

See the list below and choose ten items, putting them in descending order of importance, i.e., one for the most important and ten for the least. It doesn't matter how you arrive at your decisions but it's as important to consider what you should leave with those in the tent as it is to think about the mission.

These choices could mean the difference between survival and disaster for the members of your group. Take half an hour or forty-five minutes if working with friends to allow for discussion time.

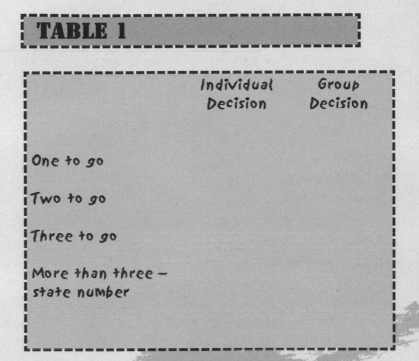

TABLE 1

	Individual Decision	Group Decision
One to go		
Two to go		
Three to go		
More than three — state number		

Fill in your answers to Table 2 on the next page without looking at the answers on the facing page. I'm trusting you not to cheat now . . . so play fair!

TABLE 2

	Individual Decision	Group Decision
Compass		
Map of area		
4 sleeping bags, summer weight		
3 packets soup		
Small first-aid kit		
Pocketknife		
2 packets fruitcake		
Matches in waterproof container		
Book entitled Advanced Scout Guide to Hiking		
4-battery flashlight		
120 ft (36 m) of 9 mm rope		
4 Snickers candy bars		
Whistle		
Watch		
1 ice ax		
Primus stove and cylinder		
Large polyethylene bag		
2 flares		
2 backpacks		

SOLUTIONS

So how did you cope? Find it hard to choose? If you did the exercise with friends, did you find it harder or easier? Learning to discuss the various options, to listen to others' viewpoints and to find ways to persuade others of the merits of your plan are all useful skills for real-life survival situations. After all, if this had been for real, you'd have had to go through the discussion process on the hillside in difficult conditions, so a bit of practice in the warmth of your bedroom can't hurt.

Table 1: Three people should go for help.

Table 2: Equipment to take in order of priority:

1. Compass: To find your way (I assume you can use it if you've got it in your kit!).
2. Map: Again, to find your way (You can read it, can't you?).
3. Flashlight: To see the map and to signal.
4. Polyethylene bag: Makes a good wind shield and protection.
5. Whistle: Distress signal. (Remember: three blasts is the universal distress signal and sound carries a long distance in the mountains.)
6. Rope: To tie your party together, if necessary. Also acts as a recovery aid if anyone falls into a gully.
7. Ice ax: Useful to feel ground in front of party as you descend. Also useful as a splint.
8. Snickers candy bars: Quick source of energy.
9. First-aid kit: Minor use but of absolutely no benefit to people in tent.
10. Backpacks: To carry equipment — and no use to people in tent.

SCORING

Add up the points for your ten answers. Add a further 25 points if you got the correct answer of three for the optimum number of people to go for help. Now check out the results.

Compass — 12 points

Map — 11 points

Flashlight — 10 points

Polyethylene bag — 9 points

Whistle — 8 points

Rope — 7 points

Ice ax — 6 points

Snickers candy bars — 5 points

First-aid kit — 4 points

Backpacks — 3 points

Sleeping bags — 2 points

Packets of soup — 2 points

Pocketknife — 2 points

Fruitcake — 2 points

Matches — 2 points

Book — 2 points

Watch — 2 points

Primus stove — 2 points

Flares — 2 points

SCORES

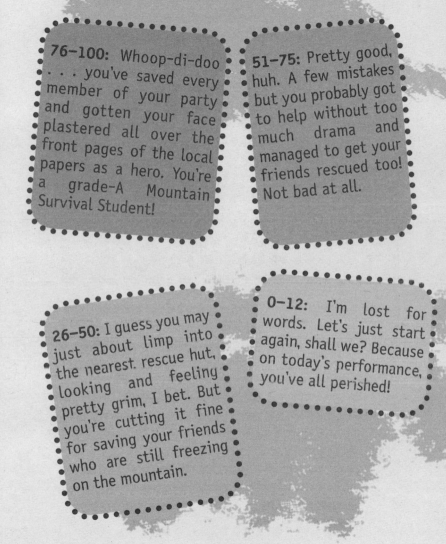

76–100: Whoop-di-doo . . . you've saved every member of your party and gotten your face plastered all over the front pages of the local papers as a hero. You're a grade-A Mountain Survival Student!

51–75: Pretty good, huh. A few mistakes but you probably got to help without too much drama and managed to get your friends rescued too! Not bad at all.

26–50: I guess you may just about limp into the nearest rescue hut, looking and feeling pretty grim, I bet. But you're cutting it fine for saving your friends who are still freezing on the mountain.

0–12: I'm lost for words. Let's just start again, shall we? Because on today's performance, you've all perished!

MOUNTAIN BEASTIES

Finally, just to keep you guessing for a while, try this frustrating mountain brainteaser!

You're having a great day out in the hills and you've stopped to eat your picnic lunch. While munching your sandwiches, you notice that there's a lot of local wildlife in the area with many attractive birds and mammals. You count 36 heads and 100 feet among them.

Assuming that birds have two feet and mammals have four, how many of each type of animal are there?

Answer:
twenty-two birds (forty-four feet) and fourteen mammals (fifty-six feet)

YOUR
MOUNTAIN
SURVIVOR'S
RATING

YOUR MOUNTAIN SURVIVOR'S RATING

It's nearly time for us to part company . . . but before we do, there's just one last thing. I couldn't let you go without that little questionnaire I promised, now could I? or you'll think I'm getting soft in my old age!

You'll be surprised at just how much valuable information you've picked up during our adventure together . . . and if you're struggling over a particular question, don't worry — just flick back over the pages because all the answers are hidden away in previous chapters.

So, find yourself a quiet corner where you won't be disturbed and settle down for your final challenge of the book. Good luck!

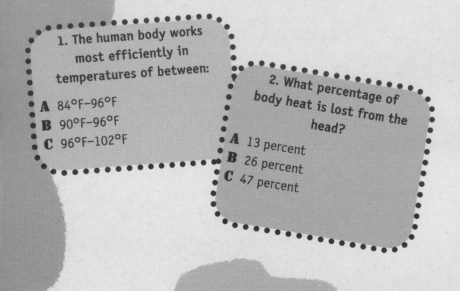

1. The human body works most efficiently in temperatures of between:

A 84°F–96°F
B 90°F–96°F
C 96°F–102°F

2. What percentage of body heat is lost from the head?

A 13 percent
B 26 percent
C 47 percent

3. When a search-and-rescue operation takes place, the internationally recognized search signal is six blasts on a whistle, wait a minute, then another six blasts. The missing person should respond with:

A three long blasts

B six long blasts

C shouts and whoops of joy

4. When taking shelter in a snow cave, you should:

A sleep on a bed of compacted snow

B sleep on a bed of leaves or branches

C sleep on a futon

5. On operations in the polar regions, the SAS dry their wet boots by:

A putting boots in the fire

B putting hot water from the fire in boots

C putting hot stones from the fire in boots

6. The word "scree" describes:

A small, loose stones

B a very steep, leeward slope

C the noise you make when you fall down a very steep, leeward slope

7. A "pulk" is another name for:

A the spots that you get when dehydrated

B a sled pulled by manpower

C a flightless Antarctic bird

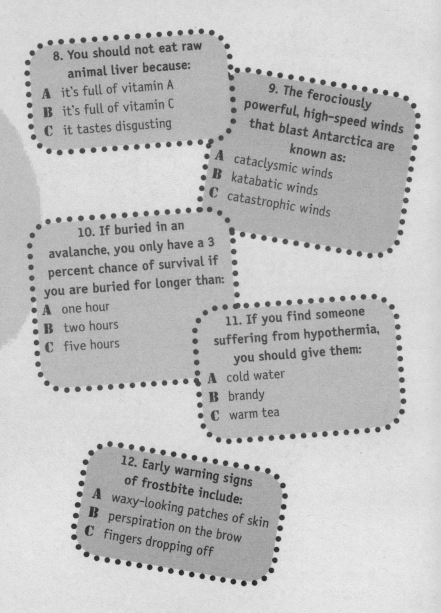

8. You should not eat raw animal liver because:

A it's full of vitamin A
B it's full of vitamin C
C it tastes disgusting

9. The ferociously powerful, high-speed winds that blast Antarctica are known as:

A cataclysmic winds
B katabatic winds
C catastrophic winds

10. If buried in an avalanche, you only have a 3 percent chance of survival if you are buried for longer than:

A one hour
B two hours
C five hours

11. If you find someone suffering from hypothermia, you should give them:

A cold water
B brandy
C warm tea

12. Early warning signs of frostbite include:

A waxy-looking patches of skin
B perspiration on the brow
C fingers dropping off

ANSWERS

1c The human body functions most efficiently when it is between 96°F–102°F (35.5°C–39°C). In temperatures above or below this, you'll find it hard to work or to function well at all.

2c Yep, remarkably, you lose nearly half your body heat through your head, so don't forget to pack a hat.

3a Whatever the signal, whether it be light, sound, or a physically laid-out message, three repeats is the universally accepted distress signal, so you would reply to the six search-and-rescue blasts with three blasts on your whistle/flashes of your flashlight, etc. You should save your whooping and hollering until you're picked up, otherwise you might be celebrating prematurely.

4b Snow conducts heat away from the body 20 times more than leaves or branches, so always make sure you're insulated from the snow when you lie down in your shelter to sleep. If you chose "futon" you'd better guess again.

5c It's tricky timing it just right so the stones don't burn your boots, but not half as perilous as putting hot water into an SAS soldier's boots — or worse still putting them on the fire. You're a braver man than me if you deliberately wreck his boots!

6a Scree is the slippery surface made up of little pebbles and stones that's so treacherous to cross when you're in the mountains. I can just imagine the kind of noise you'd make as you hurtle down a slope and it's called a "scream," not a "scree."

7b A pulk is another name for a human-pulled sled. Do you get spots when you're dehydrated? If you do, I'm sure they're not called pulks. The flightless birds you're thinking of are probably penguins . . . am I right?

8a Unfortunately, large quantities of vitamin A are poisonous to humans. But if you chose answer (c) I'll give you a bonus point because I agree with you — raw liver does taste disgusting!

9b The katabatic winds of Antarctica can rip a tent to shreds in seconds. Which I guess would be pretty cataclysmic and, indeed, catastrophic (go on — look them up in the dictionary!).

10b Your chances of survival after being buried for just two hours are very slim. That's not long, is it?

11c You should never give alcohol to someone suffering from hypothermia because it lowers body temperature still further — a glass of cold water would have a similar effect. A warm drink is your best bet.

12a A tingling sensation and waxy patches of skin are early warning signs of frostbite, whereas perspiration on the brow usually means quite the opposite, i.e., you sweat to cool your body down when you're overheating. If someone's fingers are dropping off, the frostbite is in its final stages and I would suggest that you're a bit slow in picking up the clues.

So, how did you do? I knew you could do it! A resounding success I'll wager and, if not, I'll bet you were close. With those glowing marks, you're now far better equipped to face the challenges of the mountains in the unlikely event that you find yourself stranded in the hills.

Nonetheless, it's worth bearing in mind that however invaluable these tips, you should never willingly put yourself in a position where you have to use survival skills for real. The people you've just read about in this book did not choose to find themselves in these perilous situations but they made the very best of it when they found themselves in danger. And I trust that you would do the same if you had to . . . but never, never endanger yourself unnecessarily.

Mountains and hills are dangerous and unforgiving environments and you should only venture into them in the safe hands of the experts. And who knows . . . if you get a taste for it, as I did, and you learn well, one day you, too, could be a mountain survival expert!

Until then, I hope you've enjoyed the book and that you'll find the advice helpful if you ever go searching for your own personal "gold" in the hills.